WITHDRAWN

EasyScript

EXPRESS

170201

Leonard D. Levin

TABLE OF CONTENTS

INTRODUCTION

EasyScript (ES) and Existing Shorthand Systems

All existing shorthand and speedwriting systems (except EasyScript) are based on memorizing random abbreviations.

If you use traditional methods of shorthand or speedwriting daily, it is unlikely that you will regularly use all the symbols memorized. Those that are not used daily are forgotten and cannot be remembered when needed, so proficiency declines.

The ES system is based on a concept which is easy to master and simple to transcribe. This method drastically reduces learning time, eliminates skill retention problems, increases abbreviation speed and decreases transcription time.

If you take notes on a regular basis you can adapt this method to improve your comprehension for use in school, at work, or in any other situation where note taking is important.

FAST WRITING MEANS BETTER DECISIONS

Have you thought that improving written communication between employees will enable them to make better decisions? Imagine you can put all employees on the same "page" by using one uniform system of written communications. We can train your people to perform written communications recording in a manual form and/or with computer-aided note-taking and transcription technology **(CAN/CAT).**

HALF-DAY TRAINING AND LICENSING

Follow the major U.S. companies which have licensed and implemented EasyScript/ComputerScript systems. Give us a call and we'll show you how in just a half-day we can train your employees with your choice of location, time and group size. On-site training licenses are available.

Listed below are Fortune 500 companies, government agencies and major educational institutions that offered ES/CS training programs to their employees:

> **Bell Atlantic,**
> **John Hancock Insurance,**
> **Texaco Inc.,**
> **MIT,**
> **Brandeis University,**
> **U.S. Postal Service,**
> **The Prudential Insurance,**
> **Mt. Sinai Medical Center,**
> **The Fleet Bank,**
> **U.S. Navy,**
> **NASA and many others.**

This course is also available in a classroom format for teaching the middle, high school and college students. Since 1990 students as young as 10 years of age have attended EasyScript classes and they reported that EasyScript (ES) is very useful for taking lecture notes and for reducing the volume of writing.

TRANSCRIPTION SOFTWARE

You have the option of converting notes written in ES into regular text on a PC by using **ComputerScript (CS)** software. CS enables you to enter abbreviations into a computer via the conventional keyboard. When you press a function button your abbreviations are automatically transcribed into readable text. Portable (or laptop) computer users can input their text directly using CS. ES and CS use identical rules.

NOTES PAGES

The pages marked "Notes" will help to reinforce your symbol memorization and can also be used for taking notes when you start using the method. Additional spaces are provided if you wish to add custom prefix, suffix, and prefix/suffix particles and their designations. Additional ES notepads are available and can be ordered directly from Legend Company.

Legend Company offers programs for all proficiency levels including courses for teachers and trainers to conduct classroom instruction. Higher level courses don't require purchasing a preceding level course since every course has a basic method introduction and its reinforcement.

EasyScript I (68 page book & 1 audio cassette
    20-40wpm) - beginner level
EasyScript II (128 page book & 2 audio cassettes
    20-80wpm) - intermediate level
EasyScript III (ES II book & 4 audio cassettes
    20-130wpm) - advanced/instructor level.

The following programs include ComputerScript transcription and speedtyping software which can also be purchased:

EasyScript/ComputerScript I (ES I book, 1 audio
    cassette 20-40wpm & CS software)
EasyScript/ComputerScript II (ES II book, 2 audio
    cassettes 20-80wpm & CS software)
EasyScript/ComputerScript III (ES II book, 4 audio
    cassettes 20-130wpm & CS software)
ComputerScript Software (3.5" disk & manual,
    Windows/Windows NT compatible).

THE EASYSCRIPT CONCEPT

Words are divided into five categories. ES assigns every word to one of the 5 word categories :

1) A **SIMPLE** word is a word without a prefix or suffix.

Examples: **be, and, have, able, any, should, paragraph.**

2) A **PREFIX** word has a particle before the root.

Examples: **con** as in contest, **pro** as in propose, and **under** as in understand.

3) A **SUFFIX** word has a particle after the root.

Examples: **ance** as in maintenance, **able** as in available, **er** as in manufacturer.

4) A **PREFIX-SUFFIX** word has particles both before and after the root.

Examples: **de** and **tion** as in detention, **un** and **able** as in unavoidable.

5) A **COMPOUND** word is made up of two words joined together to form another word.

Examples: **copyright, overdevelop, scorekeeper.**

NOTES

Lesson I

SIMPLE WORDS

Definition of Simple Words

A Simple Word is a word without a prefix or suffix. For short simple words EasyScript uses the Simple Rule which has two techniques: the alphabetical technique, for short simple words and the positional technique for long simple words.

In general, short words consist of one or two syllables. Long words usually consist of two or more syllables.

SIMPLE RULE

Short Words

Alphabetical Technique

Use a one, two or three-letter alphabetical code made up of letters which are part of a word or leave out all or some of the vowels.

As a rule, use 1 and 2-letter codes for higher frequency words and 3-letter codes for lower frequency words.

You can make adjustments in some instances. A higher frequency word can be abbreviated by the alphabetical technique even though the word is long. For example: the word gentlemen is abbreviated **g** as shown on page 11.

NOTES

If a given word can be abbreviated in several ways, easy memorization and fast transcription should be your determining factors.

To expand your abbreviating choices you can use the phonic technique which uses sounds associated with the word, for example, **z** = as, **k** = can.

LONG WORDS

Positional Technique

ES offers three options for using the positional technique.

First 4 - Use the first 4 letters of the word as your abbreviation.

Two + 2 - Use the first 2 letters and the last 2 letters of the word as your abbreviation.

Three + 1 - Use the first 3 letters and the last letter as your abbreviation.

Use First 4 as your **main option** and Two + 2 or Three + 1 as **alternatives** for certain words ONLY.

In certain cases, such as the words **analyze, analysis, analyst,** the First 4 rule will produce the same code for all these words. In this case, you can continue to use the First 4 rule and rely completely on context to interpret, or you can use the Two + 2 rule or Three + 1 which produces a different code for each word as an alternative.

NOTES

Material to Study

Alphabetical Technique

Write and memorize the codes in the space provided.

A. **One-letter codes** - for very high frequency words

and (**d**) _____   in (**n**) _____   the (**h**)_____

as (**z**) _____   is (**s**) _____   to (**t**) _____

be (**b**)_____   may (**m**) _____   you (**u**) _____

very (**v**) _____   gentlemen (**g**)_____

of (**o**) _____   we (**w**) _____   if (**f**) _____

B. **Two-letter codes** - for high frequency words

any (**ny**) _____   have (**hv**) _____

was (**ws**) _____   are (**ar**) _____

like (**lk**) _____   week (**wk**)_____

due (**du**) _____   new (**nw**) _____

were (**wr**) _____   for (**fr**) _____

our (**ou**) _____   will (**wl**) _____

NOTES

from (**fm**) _____ than (**tn**) _____

would (**wd**) _____ has (**hs**) _____

that (**th**) _____ your (**yr**) _____

C. **Three-letter codes** – for average frequency words

able (**abl**) _____ fill (**fll**) _____

should (**shd**) ____ about (**abt**) _____

find (**fnd**) _____ then (**thn**) _____

also (**als**) _____ firm (**frm**) _____

D. Phrases

the following (**tf**) _____

Dear Mr. (**dm**) _____

thank you (**ty**) _____

Very truly yours (**vty**) _____

Positional Technique

Write abbreviations for the following words using the rules described on page 9: **First 4** as a main option and **Two + 2** or **Three + 1** as an alternative:

NOTES

	First 4	**3+1**	**2+2**
particular	_____		
merchandise	_____		
curriculum	_____		
knowledge	_____		
analyze	_____	_____	_____
analysis	_____	_____	_____
analyst	_____	_____	_____

The codes for these words are given on page 99.

The context is always a helpful factor in the transcription process. Some abbreviations create meaningful words such as part for particular or know for knowledge. Keep in mind, if you write know or part in ES, their abbreviated form is **knw** and **prt.**

Below you can see how the codes written in context by using the **First 4, 2 + 2**, and **3 +1** rules can be easily transcribed:

This case, in particular, is very good.
Ths cse n part (parr, paar) s v gd.

This part of the movie, in particular, was very bad.
Ths prt o h movi, n part (parr, paar), ws v bd.

Many people will partake in this event.
Mny ppl wl part (pare, pake) n ths evnt.

NOTES

Merchandise was not sent on time.
Merc ws nt snt on tme.

ES enables you to abbreviate any word without exception. However, for a limited number of words you might consider using special characters, common or "buzzword" abbreviations or numerals if it makes your note-taking easier.

Special Characters

!	= exclaim;	★	=	star
=	= equal;	( )	=	bracket
$	= dollar or dollars			
>	= greater;	"	=	quote
%	= percent;	<	=	less
?	= question;	\	=	slash
.	= period;	@	=	at
+	= add, (ed, ing, tion)			
'	= not (does not = do'; have not = hv')			

Common Abbreviations

ft	= foot	**av** =	avenue
5K	= 5 thousand	**apt** =	apartment
st	= street	**hr** =	hour

Days

su	= Sunday	**mo** =	Monday
tu	= Tuesday	**wn** =	Wednesday
th	= Thursday	**fr** =	Friday
sa	= Saturday		

NOTES

Months

jan = January **feb** = February **mar**= March
apr = April **may**= May **jun** = June
jul = July **aug** = August **sep** = September
oct = October **nov** = November **dec** = December

A date can be abbreviated as follows: May 1 = **5/1**.
Geographical terms and proper names which don't have
commonly established symbols can be abbreviated by
applying the alphabetical and positional technique.

Material to Practice

Write the appropriate symbols for the words below:

in _____ was _____

to _____ yesterday (**p**) _____

your _____ with_____

we_____ until_____

wish _____ July 15th _____

you _____ the _____

as _____ hasten(**p**) _____

fill_____ goods _____

NOTES

order_____ were_____

our _____ make _____

prompt (**p**) ____ size _____

correct(**p**) _____ please _____

amount_____ find _____

for_____ send_____

great _____ wrote _____

call _____ type _____

fact _____ heard _____

Missouri _____ lost _____

bought _____ today _____

merchandise (**p**) _____

guarantee (**p**) _____

address (**p**) _____

(**p**) – the positional technique **First 4** should be used.

Check the answers on page 99.

NOTES

Prefixes

ac ap as	=	**a**	per pre pro	=	**p**	com con	=	**c**	sub sup super	=	**s**
de dis	=	**d**	tran trans	=	**t**	en	=	**e**	un under	=	**u**
ex	=	**x**	for fore	=	**f**	im in inter	=	**i**	ir re	=	**r**
_____	=	__	_____	=	__	_____	=	__	_____	=	__

Lesson 2

PREFIX WORDS

Definition of Prefix Words

Any word which has a root with a prefix particle is a prefix word. The list of frequently used prefixes is given below and they are abbreviated with one letter as shown in the parenthesis.

Write and memorize prefix symbols in the space provided :

AC,AP,AS (**a**) _____   COM,CON (**c**) ____

DE, DIS (**d**) _____   EN (**e**) _____

EX (**x**) _____   FOR, FORE (**f**) ____

IN, IM, INTER (**i**) _____

PRO, PRE, PER (**p**) _____

RE,IR (**r**) _____

SUB, SUP, SUPER (**s**) _____

TRAN, TRANS (**t**) _____

UN, UNDER (**u**) _____

NOTES

Prefixes

ac ap as	=	**a**	per pre pro	=	**p**	com con	=	**c**	sub sup super	=	**s**
de dis	=	**d**	tran trans	=	**t**	en	=	**e**	un under	=	**u**
ex	=	**x**	for fore	=	**f**	im in inter	=	**i**	ir re	=	**r**
_____	=	__	_____	=	__	_____	=	__	_____	=	__

PREFIX RULE

To abbreviate a prefix word use the prefix symbol +
SCR or OVR

EXAMPLE :

	U	1	2	3	4
UNDERSTAND > UNDER	- S	T	A	N	d

\ | | | | /   \ | | | | | /
PREFIX   ROOT

The resulting abbreviations are :

3	**4**	
USTA	USTAN	USTND

\ | | | | | | | | | | | | | /
SCR   **OVR**

THE ROOT OPTIONS

The SCR (**Straight Count Root**) starts always with
the FIRST ROOT LETTER.

1) the root is written with 3 letters (the column designated with the number 3 at the top)

2) the root is written with 4 letters (the column designated with the number 4 at the top)

3) **Omit Vowel Root** (the column designated as OVR)
is a form of abbreviation where you omit all or some of
the vowels in the root.

NOTES

Prefixes

ac ap as =	**a**	per pre pro	=	**p**	com con	=	**c**	sub sup super =	**s**
de dis =	**d**	tran trans	=	**t**	en	=	**e**	un under =	**u**
ex =	**x**	for fore	=	**f**	im in inter	=	**i**	ir re =	**r**
___ =	__	_____	=	__	_____	=	__	_____ =	__

This option is available for users who prefer writing without the vowels. The following guidelines will help you to gain better understanding of this concept:

- Before writing an actual abbreviation each prefix word MUST BE BROKEN down into a prefix and a root

- although a prefix and a root are a part of the same abbreviation they are abbreviated SEPARATELY

- the count of 3 or 4 letters DOES NOT include the prefix symbol. When you use the SCR option, always abbreviate the root starting with the FIRST root letter.

- when you use the OVR option, omit the ROOT vowels only. You should never omit the vowels when abbreviating the prefixes.

This list of prefixes has been carefully thought out and serves most people well. However if you find that using one of these symbols slows you down, choose one that facilitates your writing. For example: you can use N for "**en**" as opposed to E which is shown on the list.

Material to Study

Write one abbreviation in each column for every word using the rule:

3 <SCR> 4   OVR

p   1 2 3 4
pro - l o n g _____   _____   _____

NOTES

Prefixes

ac ap as	=	**a**	per pre pro	=	**p**	com con	=	**c**	sub sup super	=	**s**
de dis	=	**d**	tran trans	=	**t**	en	=	**e**	un under	=	**u**
ex	=	**x**	for fore	=	**f**	im in inter	=	**i**	ir re	=	**r**
_____	=	__	_____	=	__	_____	=	__	_____	=	__

x   1 2 3 4
ex - p e c t_____   _____   _____

i   1 2 3 4
in - f o r m   _____   _____   _____

r   1 2 3 4
re - q u e s t _____   _____   _____

f   1 2 3 4
for - w a r d _____   _____   _____

c   1 2 3 4
con - t e s t _____   _____   _____

d   1 2 3 4
dis - c o u n t   _____   _____   _____

e   1 2 3 4
en - c l o s e _____   _____   _____

Tcrib tf :

1. Ths syst wl iclud tf keys : rtrie, dlete, rplac, ctrol, rturn d isert. F h usr types pst h marg h txt wl ctinu on tf lne.

Pls fward h etire amt n 5 das fm h rceip o ths letter. F u do nt rspon h ownr wl istru us t begi h pcess t evic u.

The answers are given on pages 99 and 101.

NOTES

Prefixes

ac ap as	=	a	per pre pro	=	p	com con	=	c	sub sup super	=	s
de dis	=	d	tran trans	=	t	en	=	e	un under	=	u
ex	=	x	for fore	=	f	im in inter	=	i	ir re	=	r
_____	=	__	_____	=	__	_____	=	__	_____	=	__

Material to Practice

PREFIXES

Write the appropriate abbreviations for the following :

ac ap as _____   con com_____

de dis _____   for fore _____

im in inter _____   en _____

pro pre per_____   re ir _____

ex _____   un under _____

sub sup super _____   tran trans _____

PREFIX WORDS (use 3 character SCR or OVR)

com - pass_____

con - test _____

per - sonnel _____

pre - arrange_____

pro - duct _____

NOTES

Prefixes

ac ap as	= **a**	per pre pro	= **p**	com con	= **c**	sub sup super	=	**s**
de dis	= **d**	tran trans	= **t**	en	= **e**	un under	=	**u**
ex	= **x**	for fore	= **f**	im in inter	= **i**	ir re	=	**r**
_____	= __	_____	= __	_____	= __	_____	=	__

ex - pand _____

ex - cuse _____

im - pose _____

in - put _____

inter - rupt _____

re - peat _____

re - turn _____

de - termine _____

de - lay _____

dis - play _____

ac - credit _____

ap - praise _____

as - sure _____

en - close _____

for - ward _____

fore - cast _____

NOTES

Prefixes

ac ap as	=	**a**	per pre pro	=	**p**	com con	=	**c**	sub sup super	=	**s**
de dis	=	**d**	tran trans	=	**t**	en	=	**e**	un under	=	**u**
ex	=	**x**	for fore	=	**f**	im in inter	=	**i**	ir re	=	**r**
_____	=	__	_____	=	__	_____	=	__	_____	=	__

sub - divide _____

sup - pose _____

trans - port _____

tran - sit _____

un - certain _____

under - stand_____

The answers are on page 101.

NOTES

able ible = b	er or = r	sion tion =h	age ing =g	es less ous=s	ship =p
al =l	ful = f	ure =u	ance ence =c	ic =k	ant ent ness=n
ism ment= m	ate est ist = t	ive =v	cy ly ry ty =y	ize =z	ed =d
___ =_	___ =_	___ = _	___ = _	___ = _	

Lesson 3

SUFFIX WORDS

Definition of Suffix Words

Any word which has a root with a suffix particle is a suffix word. The list of frequently used suffixes is given below. They are abbreviated with one letter as shown in the parentheses.

Write and memorize the suffix symbols in the space provided :

ABLE, IBLE (**b**) _____   AGE, ING (**g**) _____

AL (**l**) _____   ANCE, ENCE (**c**) ____

ANT, ENT, NESS (**n**)_____

ATE, EST, IST (**t**) _____

ES, OUS, LESS (**s**) _____

ER, OR (**r**) _____   FUL (**f**) _____

IC (**k**) _____   ISM, MENT (**m**)_____

IVE (**v**)_____   IZE (**z**)_____

SHIP (**p**) _____   SION, TION (**h**) _____

URE (**u**) _____

NOTES

Suffixes

able ible = b	er or = r	sion tion =h	age ing =g	es less ous=s	ship =p
al = l	ful = f	ure =u	ance ence =c	ic =k	ant ent ness=n
ism ment= m	ate est ist = t	ive =v	cy ly ry ty =y	ize =z	ed =d
_____ =_	_____ =_	_____ =_	_____ =_	_____ =_	_____ = _

SUFFIX RULE

To abbreviate suffix words use the SC root or OV root + the suffix symbol

EXAMPLE :

```
              1 2 3 4          F
SUCCESSFUL  >  S U C C e s s  - FUL
               \ | | | | /      \||/
               ROOT           SUFFIX
```

The resulting abbreviations are :

```
       3      4
    SUCF  SUCCF  SCCF
    \ | | | | | | | | | /
       SCR        OVR
```

THE ROOT OPTIONS

The SCR (**Straight Count Root**) starts always with the FIRST ROOT LETTER.

1) the root is written with 3 letters (the column designated with the number 3 at the top)

2) the root is written with 4 letters (the column designated with the number 4 at the top)

3) **Omit Vowel Root** (the column designated as OVR). This option is available for users who prefer to write without the vowels. The following guidelines will help you to gain a better understanding of this concept :

NOTES

Suffixes

able ible = b	er or = r	sion tion =h	age ing =g	es less ous=s	ship =p
al = l	ful = f	ure =u	ance ence =c	ic =k	ant ent ness=n
ism ment= m	ate est ist = t	ive =v	cy ly ry ty =y	ize =z	ed =d
___ =_	___ =_	___ = _	___ = _	___ = _	

- before writing an actual abbreviation each suffix word MUST BE BROKEN down into a suffix and a root

- although a suffix and a root are a part of the same abbreviation they are abbreviated SEPARATELY

- the count of 3 or 4 letters DOES NOT include the suffix symbol. When you use the SCR option, always abbreviate the root starting with the FIRST root letter

- when you use the OVR option, omit the ROOT vowels only. You should never omit the vowels for abbreviating the suffixes

- when you use the OVR option, do not omit the vowel in the first root position. For example, if you abbreviate the word "administrator" using the OVR option and omit the vowel "a," it will make transcription more difficult.

Material to Study

Write one abbreviation in each column for every word using the rule :

	3 < SCR > 4	OVR
1 2 3 4 **r**		
f a c t - or _____	_____	_____
1 2 3 4 **g**		
m e e t - ing _____	_____	_____

NOTES

Suffixes

able ible	= b	er or	= r	sion tion	=h	age ing	=g	es less ous	=s	ship	=p
al	= l	ful	= f	ure	=u	ance ence	=c	ic	=k	ant ent ness	=n
ism ment	= m	ate est ist	= t	ive	=v	cy ly ry ty	=y	ize	=z	ed	=d
____	=__	____	=__	____	= __	____	= __	____	= __		

1 2 3 4   **u**
p l e a s - **ure**_____ _____ _____

1 2 3 4   **l**
c l a s sic - **al** _____ _____ _____

1 2 3 4   **d**
c r e d it - **ed**_____ _____ _____

1 2 3 4   **k**
d r a m at - **ic** _____ _____ _____

Tcrib tf :

1. W hv mde a diffn arram n ou rnt collh. H lettr specs th h paym penay wd b at h oph o h bnk.

Pls lt us knw h dte on whh u wl rserv h necey equim.

W smit tf list o servs avaib fr yr specl filg. Attec at h Specl Pmit Hearg d ny chans n drawgs wl b dne on an hry basi. Addiy, ths tme frme s sject t obtag dta fm yr Pject Admir r Coor. Custr mainc cn b dne at an affob rte.

                       3   4   OVR
1 2 3 4   **d**
s p e c ified - **ed** ____ _____ _____

1 2 3 4   **s**
p r i c - **es** _____ _____ _____

1 2 3 4   **s**
l i s t - **less** _____ _____ _____

NOTES

Suffixes

able ible	= b	er or	= r	sion tion	=h	age ing	=g	es less ous=s	ship	=p
al	= l	ful	= f	ure	=u	ance ence	=c	ic	=k	ant ent ness=n
ism ment	= m	ate est ist	= t	ive	=v	cy ly ry ty	=y	ize	=z	ed	=d
_____	=_	_____	=_	_____	= _	_____	= _	_____	= _	

_____

_____

_____

_____

_____

_____

_____

_____

_____

_____

_____

_____

_____

_____

_____

_____

_____

_____

_____

_____

_____

_____

_____

1 2 3 4   **s**
n u m e r - **ous** _____ _____ _____

1 2 3 4   **c**
a l l i - **ance**_____ _____ _____

1 2 3 4   **c**
e v i d - **ence** _____ _____ _____

1 2 3 4   **b**
a v a i l - **able** _____ _____ _____

1 2 3 4   **n**
d i f f er - **ent** _____ _____ _____

1 2 3 4   **n**
q u i c k - **ness**_____ _____ _____

1 2 3 4   **y**
o c c u pan - **cy**_____ _____ _____

1 2 3 4   **y**
v o l u nta - **ry**_____ _____ _____

1 2 3 4   **y**
s t a b ili - **ty** _____ _____ _____

1 2 3 4   **h**
a t t e n - **tion** _____ _____ _____

1 2 3 4   **h**
d i m e n - **sion**_____ _____ _____

NOTES

Suffixes

able ible	= b	er or	= r	sion tion	=h	age ing	=g	es less ous	=s	ship	=p
al	= l	ful	= f	ure	=u	ance ence	=c	ic	=k	ant ent ness	=n
ism ment	= m	ate est ist	= t	ive	=v	cy ly ry ty	=y	ize	=z	ed	=d
_____	=__	_____	=__	_____	= __	_____	= __	_____	= __		

1 2 3 4   **t**
e a r l i - **est** _____   _____   _____

1 2 3 4   **t**
h e s i t - **ate** _____   _____   _____

1 2 3 4   **t**
s c i e n - **ist** _____   _____   _____

1 2 3 4   **v**
t e n t at - **ive** _____   _____   _____

1 2 3 4   **m**
s h i p - **ment**_____   _____   _____

1 2 3 4   **p**
s p a c e - **ship** _____   _____   _____

Tcrib tf :

2. N answr t yr lettr o h 5th w wsh t iform u th w snt copis o yr ivoics wth ou lettr o h 25th o lst mnth.

The codes for the suffix words and transcribed text above are given on pages 101 and 103.

NOTES

_____

_____

_____

_____

_____

_____

_____

_____

_____

_____

_____

_____

_____

_____

_____

_____

_____

_____

_____

_____

_____

_____

_____

Material to Practice

SUFFIXES

Write the appropriate suffix symbols for the following :

ABLE, IBLE _____ AGE, ING _____ AL _____

ANCE, ENCE _____ ANT, ENT, NESS _____

ATE, EST, IST _____ ES, OUS, LESS _____

ER, OR _____ FUL _____ IC _____

ISM, MENT _____ IVE _____ IZE _____

SHIP _____ SION, TION _____

URE _____

SUFFIX WORDS (use 3 character SCR or OVR)

addition - al _____

sever - al _____

credit - ed _____

suggest -ed _____

NOTES

able ible = b	er or = r	sion tion =h	age ing =g	es less ous=s	ship =p
al = l	ful = f	ure =u	ance ence =c	ic =k	ant ent ness=n
ism ment= m	ate est ist = t	ive =v	cy ly ry ty =y	ize =z	ed =d
_____ =_	_____ =_	_____ = _	_____ = _	_____ = _	

bas - ed _____

advantag - es _____

pric - es _____

sampl - es _____

bottom - less _____

numer - ous _____

administrat - or _____

answ - er_____

manufactur - er _____

off - er_____

attend - ance _____

occurr - ence _____

espion - age_____

obtain - ing_____

afford - able_____

brilli - ant _____

differ - ent _____

NOTES

Suffixes

able ible = b	er or = r	sion tion =h	age ing =g	es less ous=s	ship =p
al = l	ful = f	ure =u	ance ence =c	ic =k	ant ent ness=n
ism ment= m	ate est ist = t	ive =v	cy ly ry ty =y	ize =z	ed =d
____ = _	____ = _	____ = _	____ = _	____ = _	

bitter - ness _____

efficien - cy _____

satisfacto - ry_____

opportuni - ty _____

additional - ly _____

ear - ly _____

kind - ly _____

month - ly _____

mat - ure _____

documenta - tion _____

dimen - sion _____

smart - est_____

earli - est _____

fast - est_____

separ - ate _____

psychiatr - ist _____

administrat - ive _____

NOTES

_____

_____

_____

_____

_____

_____

_____

_____

_____

_____

_____

_____

_____

_____

_____

_____

_____

_____

_____

_____

_____

_____

_____

_____

arrange - ment _____

equip - ment_____

ship - ment _____

state - ment _____

success - ful _____

characterist - ic _____

member - ship _____

The answers are on pages 103 and 105.

NOTES

Lesson 4

PREFIX/SUFFIX WORDS

Definition of Prefix/Suffix Words

Any word which has a root with a prefix and a suffix particle is a prefix/suffix word.

Prefix/Suffix Rule

To abbreviate Prefix/Suffix words use the prefix symbol + the SC root or OV root + the suffix symbol.

EXAMPLE : INTRODUCTORY >

I	1 2 3 4	Y
IN -	T R O D ucto	- TY
\\\|/	\\\| | | |/	\\\|/
PREFIX	**ROOT**	**SUFFIX**

The resulting abbreviations are:

3	
ITROY	ITRDY
SCR	**OVR**

Use 4 letter root for writing applications only (when you don't have to convert verbal information into written form).

NOTES

Prefixes					Suffixes				
ac ap as	= **a**	per pre pro	= **p**	able ible	= **b**	er or	= **r**	sion tion	= **h**
com con	= **c**	sub sup super	= **s**	age ing	= **g**	es less ous	= **s**	ship	= **p**
de dis	= **d**	tran trans	= **t**	al	= **l**	ful	= **f**	ure	= **u**
en	= **e**	un under	= **u**	ance ence	= **c**	ic	= **k**	_____	= __
ex	= **x**	_____	= __	ant ent ness	= **n**	ism ment	= **m**	_____	= __
for fore	= **f**	_____	= __	ate est ist	= **t**	ive	= **v**	_____	= __
im in inter	= **i**	_____	= __	cy ly ry ty	= **y**	ize	= **z**	_____	= __
ir re	= **r**	_____	= __	ed	= **d**	_____	= __	_____	= __

A code for prefix/suffix words includes both a prefix and suffix symbol and a 3-letter root. It is longer than the corresponding code for a prefix or suffix word. Therefore, using a 3-letter root should not affect your abbreviation speed and transcription.

Material to Study

In applying the rule use the same guidelines described in Lessons 2 and 3 for the prefix and suffix words.

		3	OVR
u 1 2 3 4 b			
un - a v o i d - able	_____	_____
x 1 2 3 4 d			
ex - h a u s t - ed	_____	_____
x 1 2 3 4 h			
ex - h i b i - tion	_____	_____
e 1 2 3 4 y			
en - t i r e - ly	_____	_____

Tcrib tf:

1. Pls b advid th z t ths dte h Buyr hs faild t rcev a mortg cmittm upn h trms specd in ∂ 38 (z xtendd by lettr agrem o 7/17/87). Acordy, f h Sellr s uwillg t xtend h mortg ctingy dte z rquesd, ths lettr shl cstit a rvocah o h agrem z pvidd. Acordy, my clin rquess an xtenh o h mortg cmittm dte t 8/4/87.

The answers are given on page 105.

NOTES

Prefixes						Suffixes					
ac ap as	= **a**	per pre pro	= **p**	able ible	= **b**	er or	= **r**	sion tion	= **h**
com con	= **c**	sub sup super	= **s**	age ing	= **g**	es less ous	= **s**	ship	= **p**
de dis	= **d**	tran trans	= **t**	al	= **l**	ful	= **f**	ure	= **u**
en	= **e**	un under	= **u**	ance ence	= **c**	ic	= **k**	_____	= __
ex	= **x**	_____	= __	ant ent ness	= **n**	ism ment	= **m**	_____	= __
for fore	= **f**	_____	= __	ate est ist	= **t**	ive	= **v**	_____	= __
im in inter	= **i**	_____	= __	cy ly ry ty	= **y**	ize	= **z**	_____	= __
ir re	= **r**	_____	= __	ed	= **d**	_____	= __	_____	= __

Material to Practice

Write the appropriate symbols for the following :

PREFIXES

ac ap as _____   com con _____

de dis _____   for fore _____

im in inter _____   en _____

pro pre per_____   re ir _____

ex _____   un under _____

sub sup super _____   tran trans _____

SUFFIXES

able ible _____   age ing _____

al_____   ance ence _____

ant ent ness_____   ate est ist _____

cy ly ty ry _____   ed _____

er or _____   es ous less _____

ful _____   ic _____

NOTES

Prefixes					Suffixes				
ac ap as	= **a**	per pre pro	= **p**	able ible =	**b**	er or	= **r**	sion tion =	**h**
com con	= **c**	sub sup super	= **s**	age ing =	**g**	es less ous =	**s**	ship	= **p**
de dis	= **d**	tran trans	= **t**	al =	**l**	ful	= **f**	ure	= **u**
en	= **e**	un under	= **u**	ance ence =	**c**	ic	= **k**	_____	= __
ex	= **x**	_____	= __	ant ent ness=	**n**	ism ment	= **m**	_____	= __
for fore	= **f**	_____	= __	ate est ist =	**t**	ive	= **v**	_____	= __
im in inter	= **i**	_____	= __	cy ly ry ty =	**y**	ize	= **z**	_____	= __
ir re	= **r**	_____	= __	ed =	**d**	_____	= __	_____	= __

ism ment _____ ive _____

ize _____ ship _____

sion tion_____ ure_____

PREFIX/SUFFIX WORDS

Determine the prefix, the suffix and the root letters of the words below and write them separately in the first column as shown in the example. It is important to learn to extract the NECESSARY letters but not the WHOLE root. Your ability to perform this extraction becomes especially critical for words with longer roots.

In the second column write a full abbreviation applying the prefix/suffix rule by using ONE 3 letter option (SCR or OVR) at a time. Use the OVR only for shorter words.

Examples : CONVENTIONAL >

1st column	2nd column
CON - VEN - AL	**CVENL**

DISAPPOINTMENT >

1st column	2nd column
DIS - APP - MENT	**DAPPM**

NOTES

Prefixes						Suffixes				
ac ap as	= **a**	per pre pro	= **p**	able ible	= **b**	er or	= **r**	sion tion	= **h**
com con	= **c**	sub sup super	= **s**	age ing	= **g**	es less ous	= **s**	ship	= **p**
de dis	= **d**	tran trans	= **t**	al	= **l**	ful	= **f**	ure	= **u**
en	= **e**	un under	= **u**	ance ence	= **c**	ic	= **k**	_____	= __
ex	= **x**	_____	= __	ant ent ness	= **n**	ism ment	= **m**	_____	= __
for fore	= **f**	_____	= __	ate est ist	= **t**	ive	= **v**	_____	= __
im in inter	= **i**	_____	= __	cy ly ry ty	= **y**	ize	= **z**	_____	= __
ir re	= **r**	_____	= __	ed	= **d**	_____	= __	_____	= __

Writing Exercise

	1st column	2nd column
conversely		
consistently		
consideration		
responsibility		
relevant		
received		
reviewing		
requested		
investigate		

Tcri tf :

1. Cvery, mst csisy sucf limd parrs acep rspoy t ivest potl genl parrs. 1 o h elems t csidr whn rvieg h stru o a limd parp s potl cfli o itert. Addy, a limd parr shl b pvid wth h rlevn info durg h lst sevl oprg qrtrs.

| intelligently | | |
| entirely | | |

NOTES

Prefixes					Suffixes				
ac ap as	= **a**	per pre pro	= **p**	able ible	= **b**	er or	= **r**	sion tion	= **h**
com con	= **c**	sub sup super	= **s**	age ing	= **g**	es less ous	= **s**	ship	= **p**
de dis	= **d**	tran trans	= **t**	al	= **l**	ful	= **f**	ure	= **u**
en	= **e**	un under	= **u**	ance ence	= **c**	ic	= **k**	_____	= __
ex	= **x**	_____	= __	ant ent ness	= **n**	ism ment	= **m**	_____	= __
for fore	= **f**	_____	= __	ate est ist	= **t**	ive	= **v**	_____	= __
im in inter	= **i**	_____	= __	cy ly ry ty	= **y**	ize	= **z**	_____	= __
ir re	= **r**	_____	= __	ed	= **d**			_____	= __

investment _____ _____

importance _____ _____

insured _____ _____

enclosed _____ _____

controlled _____ _____

controlling _____ _____

concerning _____ _____

unavoidable _____ _____

comfortable _____ _____

comply _____ _____..........

Tcri tf :

2. Sucf limd parrs ctin t wrk z itely at thr ivesms z thy did t mke thir mny n h 1st plce. T elat on ou csidh o h genl parrs iporc t yr ivesm succ, w wl nw lk int sme o h crtl aras ctrod by genl parrs. H limd parr n trn ows it t h/slf t rvie al doch d corc cary d t rais ccerg cfli abt whh he do' fel cforb.

requirement _____ _____

representative _____ _____

NOTES

Prefixes					Suffixes			
ac ap as	= **a**	per pre pro	= **p**	able ible = **b**	er or	= **r**	sion tion	= **h**
com con	= **c**	sub sup super	= **s**	age ing = **g**	es less ous	= **s**	ship	= **p**
de dis	= **d**	tran trans	= **t**	al = **l**	ful	= **f**	ure	= **u**
en	= **e**	un under	= **u**	ance ence = **c**	ic	= **k**	_____	= __
ex	= **x**	_____	= __	ant ent ness= **n**	ism ment	= **m**	_____	= __
for fore	= **f**	_____	= __	ate est ist = **t**	ive	= **v**	_____	= __
im in inter	= **i**	_____	= __	cy ly ry ty = **y**	ize	= **z**	_____	= __
ir re	= **r**	_____	= __	ed = **d**	_____	= __	_____	= __

reply _____ _____

demanding _____ _____

unsatisfactory _____ _____

deleted _____ _____

properties _____ _____

promotional _____ _____

independent _____ _____

communicated _____ _____

competitive _____ _____

important _____ _____

improvement _____ _____

exhausted _____ _____

indecisive _____ _____

instruction _____ _____

convenience _____ _____

supply _____ _____

NOTES

Prefixes

ac ap as	= a	per pre pro	= p
com con	= c	sub sup super	= s
de dis	= d	tran trans	= t
en	= e	un under	= u
ex	= x	_____	= __
for fore	= f	_____	= __
im in inter	= i	_____	= __
ir re	= r	_____	= __

Suffixes

able ible	= b	er or	= r	sion tion	= h
age ing	= g	es less ous	= s	ship	= p
al	= l	ful	= f	ure	= u
ance ence	= c	ic	= k	_____	= __
ant ent ness	= n	ism ment	= m	_____	= __
ate est ist	= t	ive	= v	_____	= __
cy ly ry ty	= y	ize	= z	_____	= __
ed	= d			_____	= __

Tcri tf :

3. H rquims o sucf rl estt parp manm ar too dmang t b
met by a parl effo. H iporn csidh s th evey cfli o itert b
thoy dclod n h offg doch. Fr xamp, it s oft mre ecol d
mre effv t hv affd cpans th ar ownd by genl parr t pvid
sers t ppers rthr thn t buy sers fm idepn cpans.

Info cvrs sch aras z occy, chans n pmotl pgra, phyl
iproms, m/plc, ecok trnds n h ara, finl posh o h parp d
plns fr nxt acty.

The codes for the words and the transcribed texts above
are given on pages 107 and 109.

Write the appropriate symbols for the following :

con – verse – ly _____

con – sistent – ly _____

com – p – ly _____

con – sidera – tion _____

re – sponsibili – ty _____

re – lev – ant _____

re – p – ly _____

re – view – ing _____

NOTES

Prefixes				Suffixes					
ac ap as	= a	per pre pro	= p	able ible	= b	er or	= r	sion tion	= h
com con	= c	sub sup super	= s	age ing	= g	es less ous	= s	ship	= p
de dis	= d	tran trans	= t	al	= l	ful	= f	ure	= u
en	= e	un under	= u	ance ence	= c	ic	= k	_____	= _
ex	= x	_____	= _	ant ent ness	= n	ism ment	= m	_____	= _
for fore	= f	_____	= _	ate est ist	= t	ive	= v	_____	= _
im in inter	= i	_____	= _	cy ly ry ty	= y	ize	= z	_____	= _
ir re	= r	_____	= _	ed	= d	_____	= _	_____	= _

re - quest - ed _____

in - vestig - ate _____

in - telligent - ly _____

sup - p - ly _____

in - vest - ment _____

im - port - ance _____

in - sur - ed _____

con - troll - ed _____

con - troll - ing _____

con - cern - ing _____

com - fort - able _____

re - quire - ment _____

re - ceiv - ed _____

re - presentat - ive _____

de - mand - ing _____

de - let - ed _____

NOTES

Prefixes								Suffixes						
ac ap as	= **a**	per pre pro	= **p**		able ible	=	**b**	er or	= **r**		sion tion	=	**h**
com con	= **c**	sub sup super	= **s**		age ing	=	**g**	es less ous	= **s**		ship	=	**p**
de dis	= **d**	tran trans	= **t**		al	=	**l**	ful	= **f**		ure	=	**u**
en	= **e**	un under	= **u**		ance ence	=	**c**	ic	= **k**		_____	=	__
ex	= **x**	_____	= __		ant ent ness	=	**n**	ism ment	= **m**		_____	=	__
for fore	= **f**	_____	= __		ate est ist	=	**t**	ive	= **v**		_____	=	__
im in inter	= **i**	_____	= __		cy ly ry ty	=	**y**	ize	= **z**		_____	=	__
ir re	= **r**	_____	= __		ed	=	**d**	_____	= __		_____	=	__

pro – perti – es _____

pro – motion – al _____

in – depend – ent _____

com – municat – ed _____

com – petit – ive _____

im – port – ant _____

im – prove – ment _____

in – decis – ive _____

in – struc – tion _____

con – veni – ence _____

in – troduc – ing _____

im – prov – ed _____

com – munica – tion _____

pro – cess – ing _____

pro – gress – ed _____

pro – ductivi – ty _____

NOTES

Prefixes					
ac ap as	= **a**	per pre pro	= **p**		
com con	= **c**	sub sup super	= **s**		
de dis	= **d**	tran trans	= **t**		
en	= **e**	un under	= **u**		
ex	= **x**	_____	= __		
for fore	= **f**	_____	= __		
im in inter	= **i**	_____	= __		
ir re	= **r**	_____	= __		

Suffixes					
able ible	= **b**	er or	= **r**	sion tion	= **h**
age ing	= **g**	es less ous	= **s**	ship	= **p**
al	= **l**	ful	= **f**	ure	= **u**
ance ence	= **c**	ic	= **k**	_____	= __
ant ent ness	= **n**	ism ment	= **m**	_____	= __
ate est ist	= **t**	ive	= **v**	_____	= __
cy ly ry ty	= **y**	ize	= **z**	_____	= __
ed	= **d**	_____	= __	_____	= __

un - success - ful _____

un - satisfacto - ry _____

de - velop - er _____

in - dic - ate _____

com - puter - ize _____

un - resolv - ed _____

un - avoid - able _____

ac - cord - ance _____

ac - knowledg - ed _____

ap - preciat - ed _____

en - clos - ing _____

en - clos - ed _____

en - tire - ly _____

ex - haust - ed _____

The answers are on pages 109 and 111.

NOTES

Lesson 5

COMPOUND WORDS

Definition of compound words

Any word which is composed of two or more words is a compound word.

COMPOUND RULES

Material to Study

Read the rules and write the appropriate abbreviations using each rule.

Simple Compound

Use the first letter of the first word followed by a slash sign (\) or (/) and up to 3 first or up to 3 non-vowel letters of the second word. The choice between (\) or (/) is available for right-handed and left-handed users.

Example:

	SCR	OVR
AIR \ CRAFT	-a\cr a\cra	a\crt

	SCR	OVR
club/house	_____	_____
copy/right	_____	_____
blood/test	_____	_____

NOTES

Suffix Compound

Use the first letter of the first word followed by a slash sign (\) or (/) and 2 first or 2 non-vowel letters of the second word + the suffix symbol.

Example:

```
         SCR      OVR
GUIDE \ LIN - ES   g\lis   g\lns
```

	SCR	OVR
peace/maker	_____	_____
photo/copying	_____	_____
how/ever	_____	_____
counter/offer	_____	_____
counter/measure	_____	_____

Prefix Compound

Use the first letter of the first word followed by a slash sign(\) or (/) and prefix symbol + 2 next or 2 non-vowel letters of the second word.

Example:

```
                    SCR  OVR
OVER \ EX - POSE -  o\xpo  o\xps
```

NOTES

	SCR	OVR
over/protect	_____	_____
over/extend	_____	_____

Prefix/Suffix Compound

Use the first letter of the first word followed by a slash sign (\) or (/) and prefix symbol, 1 root letter and suffix symbol of the second word.

Example: counterproposal

COUNTER \ PRO - POS - AL   c\ppl

over/development _____

over/production _____

counter/productive _____

The codes for the above compound words are given on pages 111 and 113.

NOTES

Material to Practice

Writing Exercise

Write the appropriate abbreviations for the words below:

Simple Compound

Example : buzzword > buzz - word : b/wo   b/wd

	SCR	OVR
bath/room	_____	_____
court/yard	_____	_____
chair/man	_____	_____
girl/friend	_____	_____
electro/therapy	_____	_____
boy/friend	_____	_____
main/stream	_____	_____
down/turn	_____	_____
down/hill	_____	_____
bench/mark	_____	_____

NOTES

class/room _____ _____

water/front _____ _____

flash/light _____ _____

there/fore _____ _____

Prefix Compound

Example:
overproduce >

over / pro – duce : o/pdu o/pdc

                            SCR   OVR

over/consume _____ _____

counter/propose _____ _____

over/develop_____ _____

Suffix Compound

Example:
headlines >

head – lin – es : h/lis h/lns

                            SCR   OVR

north/easterly _____ _____

NOTES

over/balance _____ _____

land/owner _____ _____

easy/going _____ _____

ware/house _____ _____

score/keeper _____ _____

out/rageous _____ _____

noise/maker _____ _____

electro/magnetism _____ _____

Prefix/Suffix Compound

counter/proposal _____ _____

over/confidence _____ _____

over/development _____ _____

over/extension _____ _____

over/exposing _____ _____

The codes for the compound words above are on page 113.

NOTES

EasyScript Overview

The Concept

ES method is based on assigning any word you abbreviate to one of the five following categories and utilizing five basic rules:

1) **Simple Words and Phrases**

Rule: Alphabetical or positional techniques

2) **Prefix Words**

Rule: Prefix symbol + 3 or 4 letters starting with the first root letter or omit vowel root

3) **Suffix Words**

Rule: 3 or 4 letters starting with the first root letter or omit vowel root + suffix symbol

4) **Prefix/Suffix Words**

Rule: Prefix symbol + 3 or 4 letters starting with the first root letter or omit vowel root + suffix symbol

5) **Compound Words**

Rule: the first letter of the first word followed by a slash sign and 2 or 3 letters of the second word

NOTES

Major Points to Study

a) assigning words to the proper category, identifying the word category, extracting the prefix and/or suffix, and extracting the root

b) memorizing simple word and prefix/suffix symbols

c) acquiring the skill of converting from verbal to written form if you have not been abbreviating on a regular basis prior to taking this course.

NOTES

Adapting to EasyScript

The following "tips" will help you to use ES
more efficiently.

- Avoid writing random abbreviations and use ES rules.

- Learn to identify the pauses while following a speak-
  er and to start a new sentence even though you did
  not complete the previous sentence.

- If a word can be abbreviated in several ways, use
  your common sense and logic to provide you with
  easy memorization and fast transcription.

- If you have been using so called "brief forms" from
  Gregg shorthand or your own symbols, include them
  in the simple code list without modification even
  though they are different from the ones in this book.
  Use ES rules for words you don't have rules or
  abbreviations for. This approach will provide a
  smoother transition to ES.

- For faster transcription, apply the rules in reverse.
  Replace the first and/or last character from the pre-
  fix/suffix list and match it with the root. This will
  help to transcribe quickly and correctly.

NOTES

- If you don't plan to read your notes immediately use longer roots to ensure faster transcription for writing applications (letter, phone messages, library research).

- For a limited number of words, assignment to a particular category is not obvious. Assign words to the categories that make abbreviating and transcription easier.

- If you wish to minimize the amount of memorization, write some of the 2 and 3 characters in longhand.

- If necessary, add new prefixes and suffixes and modify their designations.

- You can always build your proficiency at a gradual pace by applying one rule at a time.

- Extracting a WHOLE root for some longer words can affect your abbreviation speed. Concentrate on learning to extract THREE or FOUR root letters only as defined by the rules.

- If you did not take notes on a regular basis prior to starting this course you will have to develop an ability to convert verbal information into written form which is a skill itself. The best way to acquire this skill is by making a habit to take notes on a REGULAR basis when verbal information is presented to you.

- To avoid transcription problems, do not omit the vowel in the first position when you utilize the non-vowel option.

NOTES

Answers

LESSON 1

SIMPLE WORDS

Material To Study

Positional technique

part; merc; curr; know; anal anae anze; anal anas anis; anal anat anst.

Material To Practice

n, ws, t, yest, yr, wth, w, utl, wsh, 7/15, u, h, z, hast, fll, gds, ord, wr, ou, mke, prom, sz, corr, pls, amt, fnd, fr, snd, grt, wrt, cll, tpe, fct, hrd, MO, lst, bht, tdy, merc, quar, addr.

LESSON 2

PREFIX WORDS

Material To Study

  3   4   OVR
plon plong plng; xpec xpect xpct; ifor iform ifrm; rque rques rqst; fwar fward fwrd; ctes ctest ctst; dcou dcoun dcnt; eclo eclos ecls.

1. This system will include the following keys : retrieve, delete, replace, control, return, and insert. If the user

NOTES

types past the margin the text will continue on the following line.

Please forward the entire amount in 5 days from the receipt of this letter. If you do not respond the owner will instruct us to begin the process to evict you.

Material To Practice

Writing Exercise

Prefixes

a, c, d, f, i, e, p, r, x, u, s, t.

cpas (cpss), ctes (ctst), pson (psnn), parr, pduc (pdct), xpan (xpnd), xcus (xcse), ipos (ipse), iput (ipt), irup (irpt), rpea (rpt), rtur (rtrn), dter (dtrm), dlay (dly), dpla (dply), acre (acrd), apra (aprs), asur (asre), eclo (ecls), fwar (fwrd), fcas (fcst), sdiv (sdvd), spos (spse), tpor (tprt), tsit (tst), ucer (ucrt), usta (ustd).

The code in parenthesis is for OVR option. When one code is given SCR and OVR are the same.

LESSON 3

SUFFIX WORDS

Material to Study

3   4   OVR
facr factr factr; meeg meetg mtg; pleu pleau plsu; clal

NOTES

clasl clssl; cred credd crdd; drak dramk drmk.

1. We have made a different arrangement in our rent collection. The letter specifies that the payment penalty would be at the option of the bank.

Please let us know the date on which you will reserve the necessary equipment.

We submit the list of services available for your special filing. Attendance at the Special Permit Hearing and any changes in drawings will be done on an hourly basis. Additionally, this time frame is subject to obtaining data from your Project Administrator or Coordinator. Customer maintenance can be done at an affordable rate.

3   4   OVR
sped specd spcd; pris prics prcs; liss lists lsts; nums numes nmrs; allc allic allc; evic evidc evdc; avab avalb avlb; difn diffn dffn; quin quicn qckn; occy occuy occy; voly voluy vlny; stay staby stby; atth atteh atth; dimh dimeh dmnh; eart earlt erlt; hest hesit hstt; scit sciet scnt; tenv tenav tntv; shim shipm shpm; spap spacp spcp.

2. In answer to your letter on the 5th we wish to inform you that we sent copies of your invoices with our letter on the 25th of last month.

Writing Exercise

Suffixes

b, g, l, c, n, t, s, r, f, k, m, v, z, p, h, u.

NOTES

addl, sevl (svrl), cred (crdd), sugd (sggd), basd (bsd), advs, pris (prcs), sams (smps), bots (btts), nums (nmrs), admr, ansr, manr (mnfr), offr, attc, occc, espg, obtg, affb, brin (brln), difn (dffn), bitn (bttn), effy, saty, oppy, addy, eary, kiny (kndy), mony (mnty), matu (mtu), doch (dcmh), dimh (dmnh), smat (smrt), eart, fast (fstt), sept (sprt), psyt, admv, arrm, equm (eqpm), shim (shpm), stam (sttm), sucf (sccf), chak (chrk), memp (mmbp).

The code in parenthesis is for OVR option. When one code is given SCR and OVR are the same.

LESSON 4

PREFIX/SUFFIX WORDS

Material To Study

uavob uavoib uvdb; xhaud xhausd xhstd; xhibh xhibih xhbh; etiry etirey etry.

1. Please be advised that as to this date the Buyer has failed to receive a mortgage comitment upon the terms specified in paragraph 38 (as extended by letter of agreement of July 7, 1987). Accordingly, if the Seller is unwilling to extend the mortgage contingency date as requested, this letter shall constitute a revocation of the agreement as provided. Accordingly, my client requests an extension of the mortgage contingency date to August 4, 1987.

NOTES

Material to Practice

Prefixes

a, c d, f, i, e, p, r, x, u, s, t.

Suffixes

b, g, l, c, n, t, y, d, r, s, f, k, m, v, z, p, h, u.

Writing Exercise

con - ver - ly cvery; con - sis - ly csisy; con - sid - tion csidh; re - spo - ty rspoy; re - lev - ant rlevn; re - cv - ed rcvd; re - vw - ing rvwg; re - qst - ed rqstd; in - ves - ate ivest.

1. Conversely, most consistently successful limited partners accept responsibility to investigate potential general partners. One of the elements to consider when reviewing the structure of a limited partnership is potential conflict of interest. Additionally, a limited partner shall be provided with the relevant information during the last several operating quarters.

in - tel - ly itely; en - tire - ly etiry; in - ves - ment ivesm; im - por - ance iporc; in - sur - ed isurd; en - clo - ed eclod; con - tro - ed ctrod; con - tro - ing ctrog; con - cer - ing ccerg; un - avo - able uavob; com - for - able cforb; com - p - ly cpy.

2. Successful limited partners continue to work as intelligently as they did to make their money in the first place.

NOTES

To elaborate on our consideration of the general partners importance to your investment success, we will now look into some of the critical areas controlled by general partners. The limited partner in turn owes it to himself to review all documentation and correspondence carefully and to raise questions concerning conflict about which he does not feel comfortable.

re - qui - ment rquim; re - pre - ive rprev; re - p - ly rpy; de - man - ing dmang; un - sat - ry usaty; de - let - ed dletd; pro - per - es ppers; pro - mot - al pmotl; in - dep - ent idepn; com - mun - ed cmund; com - pet - ive cpetv; im - por - ant iporn; im - pro - ment iprom; ex - hst - ed xhstd; in - dec - ive idecv; in - str - tion istrh; con - ven - ence cvenc; sup - p - ly spy.

3. The requirements of successful real estate partnership management are too demanding to be met by a partial effort. The important consideration is that every conflict of interest should be thoroughly disclosed in the offering documentation.

For example, it is often more economical and more effective to have affiliated companies that are owned by the general partner provide services to properties rather than buy services from independent companies.

Information covers such areas as occupancy, changes in promotional program, physical improvements, market-place, economic trends in the area, financial position of the partnership and plans for next activity.

cvery (cvrsy); csisy (cssty); cpy; csidh (csdrh); rspoy (rspny); rlevn (rlvn); rpy; rvieg (rvwg); rqued (rqstd); ivest

NOTES

(ivstt); itely (itlly); spy; ivesm (ivstm); iporc (iprtc); isurd (isrd); ctrod (ctrld); ctrog (ctrlg); ccerg (ccrng); cforb (cfrtb); rquim (rqrm); rceid (rcvd); rprev (rprsv); dmang (dmndg); dletd (dltd); ppers (pprts); pmotl (pmtnl); idepn (idpnn); cmund (cmncd); cpetv (cpttv); iporn (iprtn); iprom (iprvm); idecv (idcsv); istrh; cvenc (cvnc); itrog (itrdg); iprod (iprvd); cmunh (cmnch); pcesg (pcssg); pgred (pgrsd); pducy (pdcty); usucf (usccf); usaty (ustfy); dvelr (dvlpr); idict (idct); cputz (cptrz); uresd (ursvd); uavob (uvdb); acorc (acrdc); ackd; apred (aprcd); eclog (eclsg); eclod (eclsd); etiry (etry); xhaud (xhstd).

The code in parenthesis is for OVR option. When one code is given SCR and OVR are the same.

LESSON 5

COMPOUND WORDS

Material to Study

Simple Compound

c/ho c/hs; c/ri c/rht; b/te b/tst.

Suffix Compound

p/mar p/mkr; p/cog p/cpg; h/evr; c/ofr; c/meu c/msu.

Prefix Compound

o/pte o/ptc; o/xte o/xtd.

NOTES

Prefix/Suffix Compound

o/dvm; o/pdh; c/pdv.

Material To Practice

Simple Compound

b/ro b/rm; c/ya c/yd; c/ma c/mn; g/fr g/fd; e/th; b/fr b/fd; m/st; d/tu d/tn; d/hl; b/ma b/mk; c/ro c/rm; w/fr w/ft; f/li f/lgt; t/fo t/fr.

Prefix Compound

o/csu o/csm; c/ppo c/pps; o/dve o/dvp.

Suffix Compound

n/esy; o/bac o/blc; l/owr; e/gog e/gg; w/ho w/hs; s/ker s/kpr; o/ras o/rgs; n/mar o/mkr; e/mam e/mgm.

Prefix/Suffix Compound

c/ppl; o/cfc; o/dvm; o/xth; o/xpg.

NOTES

General EasyScript Dictionary

1. Abbreviations are given using 3 letter Straight Count Root (SCR) or Omit Vowel Root (OVR).

2. Words with multiple prefixes and suffixes are given with alternative option shown in parentheses. For example, **ac-commoda-tion** abbreviated as a prefix/suffix word with 3 letter root- **acomh** and alternative option with 2 prefixes **ac** and **com: ac-com-moda-tion -acmdh**. The length of the root is reduced to 2 letters because 1 letter for the second prefix is added.

3. The category assignments in some cases for prefix/suffix words and a root choice are made at the writer's discretion. You can change them if a different category assignment or a root choice will make your writing and transcription faster.

4. Longer simple words are abbreviated with the First 4 rule. An alternative option (2+2 rule) is given if you wish to avoid using the same code for two different words.

5. If you can't create a unique abbreviation for certain words and you use one abbreviation for more than 1 word the context will help you to transcribe.

6. To abbreviate plurals add **-s** to the abbreviation.

7. For higher writing speed the length of the root can be reduced to 1 letter for the prefix/suffix words and to 2 letters for the prefix and suffix words.

KEY

c-compound word

p-prefix word

pm-prefix word with multiple prefixes

ps-prefix/suffix word

psm- prefix/suffix word with multiple prefixes and/or suffixes

s-suffix word

sm-suffix word with multiple suffixes

smp-simple word

2+2 - simple rule 2 first and 2 last letters

abandon	smp	aban
abandoned	s	abad
abandoning	s	abag
abbreviated	s	abbd
abbreviate	s	abbt
abbreviating	s	abbg
abbreviation	s	abbh
abide	smp	abd
ability	s	abiy
able	smp	abl
abnormal	s	abnl
about	smp	abt
above	smp	abv
absence	s	absc
absenteeism	s	absm
absolute	smp	abso
absorption	s	absh
abuse	smp	abs
abused	s	absd

116

abusive	s	absv
academic	s	acak
accept	p	acep
acceptable	ps	acepb
acceptance	ps	acepc
accepting ✓	ps	acepg
access	p	aces
accessibility ✓	ps	acesy
accident ✓	ps	acidn
accommodate	psm (acmdt)	acomt
accommodation	psm (acmdh)	acomh
accommodated	psm (acmdd)	acomd
accommodating	psm (acmdg)	acomg
accompany	psm (acpn)	acom
accordance	ps	acordc
according	ps	acorg
accordingly	ps	acory
action ✓	s	ach
actual	s	actl
actually ✓	s	acty
add	smp	ad
addition	s	addh
adding	s	addg
additional ✓	s	addl
administration	s	admh
administrative	s	admv
administrator	s	admr
advance ✓	s	advc
advancing	s	advg
advanced	s	advd
advice ✓	smp (adce 2+2)	advi
advise ✓	smp (adse 2+2)	advi
advisory	s	advy

adult ✓	smp	adlt
after ✓	s	aftr
agree ✓	smp	agr
agreed	s	agrd
agreeing	s	agrg
agreement	s	agrm
aggressive	s	agrv
aggression	s	agrh
aided	s	aidd
all	smp	al
allow	smp	allo
allowance ✓	s	allc
almost	smp	alm
already ✓	smp	alre
alter	s	altr
alteration	s	alth
alternative	s	altv
although	smp (algh 2+2)	alth
amount	smp	amt
amaze	smp	amz
amaze	smp	amad
amazing	s	amag
analysis	smp (anis 2+2)	anal
and	smp	d
another ✓	s	anor
answer ✓	s	ansr
answering	s	ansg
answered	s	ansd
anticipate	s	antt
anticipated	s	antd
anticipating	s	antg
anticipation	s	anth
any	smp	ny

appear	p	apea
appearance ✓	ps	apeac
appeared	ps	apead
appearing	ps	apeag
apply	ps	apy
applicable	ps	aplib
application √	ps	aplich
applied	ps	aplid
applying √	ps	aplyg
appreciable	psm (apcb)	apreb
appreciate	psm (apct)	aprect
appreciating	psm (apcg)	apreg
appreciated	psm (aprcd)	apred
appreciation	psm (apch)	apreh
apprehend	psm (aphn)	apre
apprehension	psm (aphnh)	apreh
apprehended	psm (aphnd)	apred
approach	pm (apch)	apro
approached	psm (apchd)	aprod
approaching	psm (apchg)	aprog
approaches	psm (apchs)	aprod
aptitude	smp	apti
architect	smp	arch
architectural	s	arcl
architecture	s	arcu
are	smp	ar
as	smp	z
asked	s	askd
asking	s	askg
aspect	smp	asp
associate	ps	asoct
associated	ps	asocd
associating	ps	asocg

association	ps	asoch
attend	smp	atte
attended	s	attd
attending	s	attg
attention	s	atth
authorize	s	autz
authorized	s	autd
authorizing	s	autg
authorization	s	auth
automatic	s	autk
automobile	smp	auto
avail	smp	avl
available ✓	s	avlb
availability	s	avly
back	smp	bck
bank	smp	bnk
base	smp	bse
based	s	basd
basic	s	bask
basically	sm (bsly)	basy
basis	smp	bas
because ✓	smp	bcs
be	smp	b
before	smp	bef
began	smp	bga
begin	smp	bgi
beginning	s	begg
behavior	s	behr
behavioral	s	behl
being	s	beg
believe	smp	blv
belief	smp	blf
believed	s	blvd

believing	s	blvg
below ✓	smp	blw
better	s	betr
best	smp	bst
between ✓	smp	btw
big	smp	bg
bill	smp	bl
biological	s	biol
board	smp	brd
book	smp	bk
both	smp	bth
bracket	smp	bkt
building ✓	s	bldg
built	smp	blt
business	s	busn
but	smp	bt
buyer	s	buyr
buzzword	c	b/wd
call	smp	cl
came	smp	cam
can	smp	cn
capability	s	capy
care	smp	cre
capital	s	capl
capitalization	sm (cplh)	caph
capitalized	sm (cpld)	capd
caring	s	carg
cared	s	card
careful	s	carf
carefully ✓	s	cary
case	smp	cse
catalog	smp	cata
catastrophic	s	catk

catastrophically	sm (ctly)	caty
central	s	cenl
centrally	sm (cntly)	ceny
centralize	sm (cntlz)	centz
centralized	sm (cnld)	cend
center	s	cenr
centered	sm (cnrd)	cend
change	snp	chg
changed	s	chgd
changing	s	chgg
character	s	char
characteristic	s	chak
characterization	sm (chrh)	chah
check	smp	chk
checking	s	chkg
checked	s	chkd
child ✓	smp	chl
children	smp	chd
chip	smp	chp
choice✓	smp	chc
choose✓	smp	cho
chose	smp	chs
choosing	s	chsg
chronic	s	chrk
circumstance	s	circ
clarify	smp	cla
clarification	s	clah
client✓	s	cln
code	smp	cde
color	s	clr
combination	ps	cbinh
come	smp	com
coming	s	comg

commercialize	psm	(cmrlz)	cmerz
commercialization	psm	(cmrlh)	cmerh
commit	p		cmit
committed	ps		cmitd
commitment	ps		cmitm
committee	p		cmit
common	p		cmon
commonly	ps		cmony
communicate✓	ps		cmunt
communicated	ps		cmund
communicating	ps		cmung
communication	ps		cmunh
community ✓	ps		cmuny
company	p		cpan
comply	ps		cpy
complex	p		cplx
compose	p		cpos
composed	ps		cposd
composer	ps		cposr
comprehend	pm	(cphn)	cpre
comprehension	psm	(cphnh)	cpreh
computer	ps		cputr
computerize	psm	(cptrz)	cputz
computerization	psm	(cptrh)	cputh
concept	p		ccep
conceptualization	psm	(cptlh)	cceph
conceptualize	psm	(cptlz)	ccepz
condition	ps		cdih
condominium	p		cdon
confirm	p		cfir
conflict	p		cfli
conscience	ps		csci
contact	p		ctac

contacted	ps	ctacd
contacting	ps	ctacg
consider	ps	csidr
considered	ps	csidd
considering	psm (csdrg)	csidg
consideration	psm (csdrh)	csidh
constitute	p	csti
constitution	ps	cstih
constitutional	psm (csthl)	cstil
contain	p	ctai
contingency	ps	ctiny
continue	p	ctin
contribute	p	ctri
contributed	ps	ctrid
contributing	ps	ctrig
contributor	ps	ctrir
contribution	ps	ctrih
control	p	ctrl
controlled	ps	ctrod
controlling	ps	ctrog
controversy	pm (ctrr)	ctro
converse	p	cver
controversial	psm (ctrrl)	ctrol
conversation	ps	cvrsh
conversion	ps	cverh
convert	p	cvrt
converted	ps	cvrtd
convertible	ps	cvrtb
converting	ps	cvrtg
copy	smp	cpy
copied	s	copd
copying	s	copg
copyright	c	c/rt

cost	smp	cst
could	smp	cld
council	smp	coun
count	smp	cnt
counted	s	cntd
counting	s	cntg
counter	s	cntr
current	smp	curr
currently	s	cury
custom	smp	cust
customer	s	custr
customize	s	cusz
data	smp	dta
database	c	d/bs
date	smp	dte
decade	smp	dcd
decide ✓	p	dcid
decided ✓	ps	dcid
deciding	ps	dcidg
decision ✓	ps	dcih
decry	p	dcry
define	p	dfin
defined	ps	dfind
defining	ps	dfing
definite	p	dfnt
definitely	ps	dfiny
definition	ps	dfinh
delay	p	dlay
delete	p	dlet
deleted ✓	ps	dletd
deleting	ps	dletg
deletion	ps	dleh
depress	pm (dpss)	dpre

depression	psm (dpsh)	dpreh
depressed	psm (dpsd)	dpred
depressing	psm (dpsg)	dpreg
demobilize	ps	dmobz
demobilization	ps	dmobh
describe	p	dscr
described	ps	dscrd
describing	ps	dscrg
description	ps	dscrh
design	p	dsig
designed	ps	dsigd
designing	ps	dsigg
designate	ps	dsigt
designated	ps	dsgnd
designating	ps	dsgng
designation	ps	dsgnh
determine	p	dter
determined	ps	dterd
determining	ps	dterg
determination	ps	dterh
develop	p	dvel
developed	ps	dveld
developer	ps	dvelr
developing	ps	dvelg
development	ps	dvelm
dictation	s	dich
dictated	s	dicd
dictating	s	dicg
dictator	s	dicr
did	smp	dd
differ	s	difr
different √	s	difn
differently	s	dify

directory	s	diry
disagree	p	dagr
disagreeing	ps	dagrg
disagreed	ps	dagrd
disagreement	ps	dagrm
discharge	p	dcha
discharged	ps	dchad
discharging	ps	dchag
discuss	p	dcus
discussed	ps	dcusd
discussing	ps	dcusg
discussion	ps	dcush
disorder	ps	dordr
disorganize	ps	dorgz
disorganized	ps	dorgd
display	p	dpla
displayed	ps	dplad
displaying	ps	dplag
disqualify	p	dqua
disqualified	ps	dquad
disqualification	ps	dquah
disturb	p	dstu
disturbance	ps	dstuc
does	smp	ds
doing	s	dog
done	smp	dn
down	smp	dwn
due	smp	du
duplicate	s	dupt
duplicated	s	dupd
duplicating	s	dupg
duplication	s	duph
during	s	durg

each	smp	ea
earlier	s	earr
early	s	ery
easier	s	easr
easy	smp	esy
edit	smp	edt
edited	s	edid
editing	s	edig
editor	s	edir
educate	s	edut
educated ✓	s	edud
educating ✓	s	edug
education ✓	s	eduh
effective ✓	s	effv
effort ✓	smp	effo
emphasize	s	empz
emphasized	s	empd
emphasizing	s	empg
emphasis	smp	emph
enclose	p	eclo
enclosed	ps	eclod
enclosing	ps	eclog
enclosure	ps	eclou
encyclopedia	p	ecly
encompass	pm	(ecps)	ecom
engineer	sm	engr
engineered	sm	(enrd)	engd
engineering	sm	(enrg)	engg
enhance	ps	ehc
enhanced	ps	ehncd
enhancing	ps	ehncg
enhancement	psm	(echm)	ehncm
enter	ps	(etrd)	etr

entered	psm (etrd)	eterd
entering	psm (etrg)	eterg
entrance	ps	etrc
entry	ps	ety
episode	smp	epis
equip	smp	eqp
equipped	s	eqpd
equipment	s	eqpm
error	s	err
essential	s	essl
essentially	s	essy
evaluate	s	evat
evaluated	s	evad
evaluating	s	evag
evaluation	s	evah
even	smp	ev
event	smp	evn
evidence✓	s	evic
example ✓	smp	exmp
exemplify	smp	exem
excess	p	xces
exchange ✓	p	xcha
exchanged	ps	xchad
exchanging	ps	xchag
excuse	p	xcus
excused	ps	xcusd
exhaust	p	xhst
exhausted	ps	xhstd
exhausting	ps	xhstg
exhaustion	ps	xhsh
exhibit	p	xhib
exhibited	ps	xhibd
exhibiting	ps	xhibg

exhibition	ps	xhibh
exist	smp	exst
existence	s	exsc
existed	s	exsd
existing	s	exsg
expand	p	xpan
expanded	ps	xpand
expanding	ps	xpang
expansion	ps	xpanh
experience	s	expc
explain	p	xpla
explained	ps	xplad
explaining	ps	xplag
explanation	ps	xplah
explanatory	ps	xplay
expert	p	xper
export	p	xpor
exported	ps	xpord
exporting	ps	xporg
extend	p	xten
extended	ps	xtend
extending	ps	xteng
extension	ps	xtenh
extinguish	p	xtin
extinguisher	ps	xtinr
fact	smp	fct
fail	smp	fl
failed	s	fld
failing	s	flg
failure	s	failu
fast	smp	fst
faster	s	fstr
feature	s	featu

field	smp	fld
file	smp	fil
find	smp	fnd
finding	s	fing
first	smp	1st
five	smp	5
follow	smp	foll
followed	s	fold
following	s	folg
for	smp	fr
foreclose	p	fclo
foreclosed	ps	fclod
foreclosure	ps	fclou
form	smp	frm
formalization	psm	(fmlzh)	fmalh
formalize	psm	(fmlz)	fmalz
formalizing	psm	(fmlzg)	fmalg
format	p	fmat
formatted	ps	fmatd
formatting	ps	fmatg
forth	smp	fth
fortitude	p	ftit
forward	p	fwar
forwarded	ps	fward
forwarding	ps	fwarg
found	smp	foun
four	smp	4
frame	smp	frme
framed	s	frmd
framing	s	frmg
freedom	smp	frdm
frequency	s	frey
frequent	s	frqn

frequently	s	frqy
friend	smp	frnd
friendship	s	frnp
from	smp	fm
function	s	funh
functional	sm (fnhl)	funl
functioned	sm (fnhd)	fund
functioning	sm (fnhg)	fung
further	s	furr
future	s	futu
gain	smp	gn
general	s	genl
generalize	sm (gnlz)	genz
generalization	sm (gnlh)	genh
genetic	s	genk
get	smp	gt
getting	s	getg
give	smp	gv
given	smp	gvn
going	s	gog
good	smp	gd
goodwill	c	g/wl
gotten	smp	gtn
grammar	smp	gram
gravitate	s	grat
gravitated	s	grad
gravitating	s	grag
gravitational	sm (grhl)	gral
great	smp	grt
greater	s	grer
group	smp	grp
guaranty	s	guay
had	smp	hd

half	smp	hlf
has	smp	hs
have	smp	hv
having	s	hvg
help	smp	hlp
helped	s	hlpd
helpful	s	hlpf
helping	s	hlpg
here	smp	hre
high	smp	hi
highlight	c	h/lt
history	s	hisy
historical	s	hisl
historically	sm (hsly)	hsty
hope	smp	hpe
hoped	s	hopd
hopeful	s	hopf
hopefully	sm (hpfy)	hopy
hoping	s	hopg
how	smp	hw
however	c	h/evr
hyphen	smp	hyph
hypnosis	smp	hypn
identify	smp	iden
identification	s	ideh
identified	s	ided
identiying	s	ideg
if	smp	f
immediate	ps	imedt
immediately	psm (imdty)	imedy
immobilize	ps	imobz
implement	ps	iplem
implementation	ps	ipleh

implemented	ps	ipled
implementing	ps	ipleg
import	p	ipor
imported	ps	ipord
importing	ps	iporg
important ✓	ps	iporn
importantly	ps	ipory
improve	pm	(ipve)	ipro
improved	psm	(ipvd)	iprod
improving	psm	(ipvg)	iprog
improvement ✓	psm	(ipvm)	iprom
in	smp		n
incidence	ps	icidc
include	p	iclu
included	ps	iclud
including	ps	iclug
inclusion	ps	icluh
income	p	icom
incomprehensive	psm	(icphv)	icomv
incomprehensibly	psm	(icphy)	icomy
incorrect	p	icor
increase	p	icre
increased	ps	icred
increasing	ps	icreg
indicate	ps	idict
indicated	ps	idicd
indicating	ps	idicg
indication	ps	idich
individual	ps	idivl
individualize	psm	(idvlz)	idivz
individualized	psm	(idvld)	idivd
industrialize	psm	(idslz)	idusz
industrialized	psm	(idsld)	idusd

industry	ps		idusy
inform	pm	(ifm)	ifor
informed	psm	(ifrmd)	iford
information √	psm	(ifrmh)	iforh
informative	psm	(ifrmv)	iforv
input	p		iput
insert	p		iser
inserted	ps		iserd
inserting	ps		iserg
insertion	ps		iserh
insurance	ps		isurc
integrate	ps		itegt
integrated	ps		itegd
integrating	ps		itegg
integration	ps		itegh
interchangeable	ps		ichab
intercourse	p		icou
interest	s		intt
interested	s		intd
interesting	s		intg
into	smp		int
introduce	p		itro
introduced	ps		itrod
introducing	ps		itrog
introduction	ps		itroh
invest	p		ives
invested	ps		ivesd
investing	ps		ivesg
investment	ps		ivesm
involve	p		ivol
involved √	ps		ivold
involving	ps		ivolg
involvement	ps		ivolm

is	smp	s
issue	smp	iss
issuable	s	issb
job	smp	jb
just	smp	jst
justification	s	jush
justify	smp	just
justified	s	jusd
justifying	s	jusg
keep	smp	kp
keeping ✔	s	kpg
key	smp	ky
kind	smp	knd
kindly	s	kiny
know	smp	knw
knowing √	s	knog
knowingly	sm (kngy)	knoy
knowledge √	smp	know
lack	smp	lck
lacking	s	lacg
lacked	s	lacd
language	smp	lang
last	smp	lst
later	s	latr
learn ✔	smp	lrn
learned ✔	s	lrnd
learning	s	lrng
lease	smp	lse
leased	s	lsd
leasing	s	lsg
leave	smp	lve
leaven	smp	lvn
leaving	s	lvg

left	smp	lft
less	smp	lss
letter	s	letr
level	smp	lvl
life	smp	lfe
like	smp	lke
likely	s	liky
liked	s	likd
liking	s	likg
limit✓	smp	lmt
limited ✓	s	limd
limiting	s	limg
limitation	s	limh
line	smp	lne
lined	s	lind
lining	s	ling
list ✓	smp	lis
listed ✓	s	lisd
listing	s	lisg
loan	smp	ln
logic	s	logk
logical	s	logl
logically	sm (lgly)	logy
long	smp	lng
longer	s	lonr
longing	s	long
look	smp	lk
looked	s	lkd
looking	s	lkg
lose	smp	ls
lot	smp	lt
machine	smp	mach
made	smp	mde

mail	smp	ml
mailing	s	mlg
mailed	s	mld
maintain	smp	main
maintenance	s	mntc
maintained	s	mntd
maintaining	s	mntg
major	s	majr
make	smp	mke
making	s	makg
manage	s	mng
managed	s	mngd
managing	s	mngg
management	s	mngm
manual	s	manl
manufacture	s	manu
manufactured	s	mand
manufacturer	s	manr
manufacturing	s	mang
many	smp	mny
margin	smp	marg
market	smp	mkt
marketer	s	mktr
marketed	s	mktd
marketing	s	mktg
master	s	masr
mastered	sm (msrd)	masd
mastering	sm (msrg)	masg
may	smp	m
mean	smp	mn
meaning	s	mng
member	s	memr
membership	s	memp

memory	s	memy
mental	s	mntl
mentally	sm (mnly)	meny
mention	s	menh
mentioned	sm (mnhd)	mend
mentioning	sm (mnhg)	meng
method	smp	meth
might	smp	mht
mind	smp	mnd
mode	smp	mde
modern	smp	mode
month	smp	mo
monthly	s	moy
more	smp	mre
mortgage	s	mrtg
most	smp	mst
move	smp	mve
much	smp	mch
multiple	smp	mult
must	smp	mst
name	smp	nme
namely	s	namy
necessary	s	necy
need	smp	nd
needed	s	ndd
new	smp	nw
next	smp	nxt
not	smp	nt
note	smp	nte
noted	s	notd
noting	s	notg
notice	smp	noti
noticed	s	ntcd

noticing	s	ntcg
number	s	numr
numerous	s	nums
obligate	s	oblt
obligated	s	obld
obligation	s	oblh
obtain	smp	obt
obtained	s	obtd
obtaining	s	obtg
occur	smp	occ
occurrence	s	occc
occurred	s	occd
occurring	s	occg
of	smp	o
off	smp	of
offer	ps	ofr
offered	s	offd
offering	s	offg
office	smp	ofc
often	smp	oft
oldest	s	oldt
one	smp	1
only	smp	onl
operate	s	opet
operated	s	oped
operating	s	opeg
operation	s	opeh
operative	s	opev
opponent	s	oppn
oppose	smp	opp
opposed	s	oppd
opposing	s	oppg
opposition	s	opph

order	smp	ord
opportunity	s	oppy
option	s	oph
ordered	s	ordd
ordering	s	ordg
organization	s	orgh
organize	s	orgz
organized	s	orgd
organizer	s	orgr
organizing	s	orgg
other	s	othr
over	smp	ovr
ownership	s	ownp
page	smp	pg
paged	s	pagd
pager	s	pagr
paging	s	pagg
paper	s	papr
paragraph	smp	para
part	smp	prt
participant	s	prtn
participate	s	prtt
participated	s	prtd
participating	s	prtg
particular	smp	part
particularly	s	prty
partner	s	prtr
partnership	sm (prrp)	prtp
past	smp	pst
paying	s	payg
payment	s	paym
people	smp	ppl
perform	pm (pfm)	pfor

performance	psm (pfmc)	pforc
performed	psm (pfmd)	pford
performing	psm (pfmg)	pforg
person	p	pson
personal	ps	psonl
personality	psm (psnly)	psony
personalize	psm (psnlz)	psonz
personalized	psm (psnld)	psond
personnel	p	psnn
persuade	p	psua
persuaded	ps	psuad
persuading	ps	psuag
persuasive	ps	psuav
phrase	smp	phr
physical	s	phyl
physically	sm (phly)	phyy
plan	smp	pln
planned	s	plnd
planner	s	plnr
planning	s	plng
please	smp	pls
population	s	poph
portion	s	porh
possible	s	posb
possibly	s	posy
position	s	posh
positioned	sm (pshd)	posd
positioning	sm (pshg)	posg
potential	s	potl
potentially	sm (ptly)	poty
practical	s	prcl
practically	sm (prly)	pray
practice	smp	prac

practiced	s	prcd
practicing	s	prcg
predefine	pm (pdfn)	pdef
predefined	psm (pdfnd)	pdefd
predetermine	pm (pdtm)	pdet
predetermined	psm (pdtmd)	pdetd
preference	ps	pferc
prefix	p	pfix
premise	p	pmis
prepare	p	ppar
preparation	ps	pparh
prepared	ps	ppard
preparing	ps	pparg
present	ps	psn
presence	ps	psc
press	smp	prs
pressed	s	prsd
pressing	s	prsg
previous	ps	pvis
previously	psm (pvsy)	pvisy
print	smp	prn
printed	s	prnd
printer	s	prnr
printing	s	prng
private	s	prvt
privately	sm (prty)	prvty
problem	p	pble
problematic	ps	pblek
proceed	p	pcd
proceeding	ps	pcdg
process	p	pces
processed	ps	pcesd
processing	ps	pcesg

processor	ps	pcesr
produce	p	pduc
produced	ps	pducd
producer	ps	pducr
producing	ps	pducg
product	p	pdct
production	ps	pdch
productivity	ps	pdcty
profit	p	pfit
profitable	ps	pfitb
program	p	pgra
programmed	ps	pgrad
programmer	ps	pgrar
programming	ps	pgrag
project	p	pjec
projected	ps	pjecd
projecting	ps	pjecg
pronounce	p	pnou
pronounced	ps	pnoud
pronunciation	ps	pnouh
propaganda	p	ppag
property	ps	ppery
prosecute	p	psec
prosecuted	ps	psecd
prosecuting	ps	psecg
prosecutor	ps	psecr
protect	p	ptec
protected	ps	ptecd
protecting	ps	ptecg
protection	ps	ptech
provide	p	pvid
provided	ps	pvidd
providing	ps	pvidg

provision	ps	pvih
proof	smp	prf
prove	p	pven
proved	ps	prvd
proven	p	pvn
proving	ps	pvg
psychiatric	s	psyk
psychiatrist	s	psyt
public	s	pubk
publicly	s	puby
punish	smp	puni
punished	s	pund
punishing	s	pung
punishment	s	punm
put	smp	pt
putting	s	putg
question	s	queh
questioned	s	qued
questioning	s	queg
quick	smp	qck
quickly	s	qcky
rack	smp	rck
rate	smp	rte
rated	s	ratd
rating	s	ratg
rather	s	rthr
react	p	rct
reacted	ps	rctd
reacting	ps	rctg
reaction	ps	rch
read	smp	rd
readable	s	rdb
reading	s	rdg

real	smp	rl
really	s	rly
reason	smp	rsn
reasoning	s	rsng
receipt	smp	rcpt
receive	smp	rcv
received	s	rcvd
receiving	s	rcvg
recent	smp	rcn
recently	s	rcny
recommend	pm (rcmn)	rcom
recommended	psm (rcmnd)	rcomd
recommending	psm (rcmng)	rcomg
recommendation	psm (rcmnh)	rcomh
reduce	p	rduc
reduced	ps	rducd
reducing	ps	rducg
reduction	ps	rduch
referendum	smp	rfdm
refer	ps	rfr
referred	ps	rfrd
reference	ps	rfrc
referring	ps	rfrg
regard	p	rgar
regarded	ps	rgard
regarding	ps	rgarg
relate	ps	rlt
related	ps	rltd
relating	ps	rltg
relation	ps	rlh
relationship	sm (rlhp)	rltp
remember	ps	rmemr
remembered	psm (rmrd)	rmemd

remembering	psm (rmrg)	rmemg
remembrance	ps	rmemc
rent	smp	rnt
rental	s	rntl
rented	s	rntd
renting	s	rntg
repeat	p	rpt
repeated	ps	rptd
repeating	ps	rptg
replace	p	rpla
replaced	ps	rplad
replacing	ps	rplag
replacement	ps	rplam
reply	ps	rpy
replied	ps	rpld
report	p	rpor
reported	ps	rpord
reporter	ps	rporr
reporting	ps	rporg
request	p	rque
requested	ps	rqued
requesting	ps	rqueg
research	p	rsch
researched	ps	rschd
researcher	ps	rschr
researching	ps	rschg
require	p	rqui
required	ps	rquid
requiring	ps	rquig
requirement	ps	rquim
resonate	s	rsnt
resolve	p	rslv
resolved	ps	rslvd

resolving	ps	rslvg
resolute	p	rslt
resolution	ps	rslh
resource	p	rsrc
respect	p	rspe
respected	ps	rsptd
respecting	ps	rsptg
respective	ps	rsptv
respond	p	rspn
responded	ps	rspnd
responding	ps	rspng
response	p	rspn
result	p	rsul
resulted	ps	rsuld
resulting	ps	rsulg
retain	p	rtn
retained	ps	rtnd
retainer	ps	rtnr
retaining	ps	rtng
retrieval	ps	rtril
retrieve	p	rtri
retrieved	ps	rtrid
retrieving	ps	rtrig
return	p	rtur
returned	ps	rturd
returning	ps	rturg
retype	p	rtyp
retyped	ps	rtypd
retyping	ps	rtypg
review	p	rvw
reviewed	ps	rvwd
reviewer	ps	rvwr
reviewing	ps	rvwg

revocation	ps	rvoch
revolution	ps	revh
revolutionary	psm (rvlhy)	rvly
revolutionize	psm (rvlhz)	rvlz
revolutionizing	psm (rvlhg)	rvlg
right	smp	rt
risk	smp	rsk
risked	s	rskd
risking	s	rskg
risky	smp	rsky
room	smp	rm
root	smp	rt
rooted	s	rtd
rooting	s	rtg
rule	smp	rle
ruled	s	ruld
ruling	s	rulg
said	smp	sd
same	smp	sme
satisfy	smp	sat
satisfactory	s	saty
satisfied	s	satd
satisfying	s	satg
save	smp	sve
saved	s	savd
saving	s	savg
serve	smp	srv
served	s	srvd
serving	s	srvg
server	s	srvr
saying	s	sayg
second	smp	sec
see	smp	c

seeing	s	seeg
seen	smp	sn
self	smp	slf
sell	smp	sll
seller	s	sllr
selling	s	sllg
separate	s	sept
separated	s	sepd
separating	s	sepg
separation	s	seph
series	s	srs
service	smp	svc
serviced	s	svcd
servicing	s	svcg
set	smp	st
setting	s	sttg
several	s	sevl
sex	smp	sx
sexual	s	sxl
sexuality	sm (sxly)	sexy
shall	smp	shl
shallow	smp	shal
ship	smp	shp
shipped	s	shpg
shipping	s	shpg
shipment	s	shpm
shorthand	c	s/hd
shorthanded	c	s/hdd
should	smp	shd
show	smp	shw
showed	s	shwd
showing	s	shwg
shown	smp	shwn

sign	smp	sgn
signal	s	sigl
signaled	sm (sgld)	sigd
signed	s	sigd
signing	s	sigg
significant	s	sign
significantly	sm (sgny)	sigy
similar	smp	simi
similarly	s	simy
simple	smp	sim
simplify	smp	simp
simplified	s	simd
simplifying	s	simg
simplicity	s	smpy
simulate	s	simt
simulated	s	smld
simulating	s	smlg
simulation	s	smlh
since	smp	snc
single	smp	sngl
size	smp	sz
sketch	smp	skt
skill	smp	skl
skilled	s	skld
sleep	smp	slp
small	smp	sml
smaller	s	smlr
smallest	s	smlt
social	s	socl
socialize	sm (sclz)	socz
socially	sm (scly)	socy
solution	s	solh
some	smp	sm

sometime	c	s/tm
sort	smp	srt
sorted	s	srtd
sorting	s	srtg
speak	smp	spk
speaker	s	spkr
speaking	s	spkg
special	s	spcl
specially	sm (sply)	spcy
specific	s	spck
specifically	sm (spfly)	spcy
specify	smp	spc
specified	s	spcd
specifying	s	spcg
staff	smp	stf
staffed	s	stfd
staffing	s	stfg
standard	smp	stnd
standardize	s	stnz
standardization	s	stnh
start	smp	strt
started	s	strtd
starting	s	strtg
state	smp	stt
stated	s	sttd
stating	s	sttg
statement	s	sttm
status	smp	stat
statistic	s	sttk
step	smp	stp
stepped	s	stpd
stepping	s	stpg
still	smp	stl

store	smp	str
storage	s	strg
stored	s	strd
storing	s	strg
structure	s	stru
study	smp	stud
studied	s	studd
studying	s	studg
subcommittee	pm (scmt)	scom
subcontract	pm (sctr)	scon
subdivide	p	sdiv
subdivided	ps	sdivd
subdividing	ps	sdivg
subdivision	ps	sdivh
subject	p	sjec
subjected	ps	sjecd
subjecting	ps	sjecg
substance	ps	sstc
substantial	ps	sstnl
substantially	psm (sstly)	sstny
success	smp	suc
successful	s	sucf
successfully	sm (scfy)	sucy
such	smp	sch
sudden	smp	sudd
suddenly	s	sudy
suffix	smp	suf
suggest	smp	sug
suggested	s	sugd
suggesting	s	sugg
suggestion	s	sugh
suicide	smp	scd
supermarket	p	smkt

support	p	spor
supported	ps	spord
supporting	ps	sporg
supreme	smp	spm
sure	smp	su
symbol	smp	symb
synopsis	smp	syno
synthesis	smp	synt
system	smp	syst
systematic	s	sysk
systemize	s	sysz
systemized	s	sysd
table	smp	tb
take	smp	tke
taken	smp	tkn
taking	s	takg
talk	smp	tlk
talked	s	tlkd
talking	s	tlkg
task	smp	tsk
team	smp	tm
teammate	c	t/mt
technical	s	tecl
technology	smp	tech
technological	s	tchl
teen	smp	tn
tenant	s	tenn
tenure	s	tenu
term	smp	trm
terminate	s	trmt
terminated	s	trmd
terminating	s	trmg
termination	s	trmh

test	smp	tst
tested	s	tstd
testing	s	tstg
text	smp	txt
than	smp	tn
that	smp	tht
the	smp	h
their	smp	thr
them	smp	thm
then	smp	thn
theory	smp	theo
there	smp	thre
these	smp	ths
thesis	smp	thes
they	smp	thy
thing	smp	thg
think	smp	thk
thinker	s	thkr
thinking	s	thkg
third	smp	3rd
thirteen	smp	13
this	smp	thi
those	smp	thos
thought	smp	thgt
thoughtful	s	thgf
thoughtfully	sm (thfy)	thoy
thousand	smp	1k
treat	smp	trt
treated	s	trtd
treatment	s	trtm
three	smp	3
threshold	c	t/hd
through	smp	thu

time	smp	tm
to	smp	t
together	smp	tgr
took	smp	tk
tool	smp	tl
train	smp	trn
trainer	s	trnr
training	s	trng
transcribe	p	tscr
transcribed	ps	tscrd
transcriber	ps	tscrr
transcribing	ps	tscrg
transcription	ps	tscrh
transform	pm (tfm)	tfor
transformed	psm (tfmd)	tford
transforming	psm (tfmg)	tforg
transformation	psm (tfmh)	tforh
transit	p	tsit
transition	ps	tsih
transport	p	tpor
transported	ps	tpord
transporting	ps	tporg
transportation	ps	tporh
trauma	smp	tma
traumatic	s	trmk
traumatize	s	trmz
tried	s	trd
truly	s	truy
trying	s	tryg
type	smp	tpe
typed	s	typd
typing	s	typg
typist	s	typt

unavoidable	ps	uavob
uncertain	p	ucer
uncommon	pm (ucmn)	ucom
under	ps	udr
underline	p	ulin
underlined	ps	ulind
underlining	ps	uling
understand	p	usta
understanding	ps	ustag
understandable	ps	ustab
unit	smp	unt
unknown	p	ukno
unsuccessful	ps	usucf
unresolved	ps	uresd
until	p	utl
unwilling	ps	uwilg
upon	smp	upn
usage	s	usg
used	s	usd
user	s	usr
using	s	usg
utility	s	utiy
utilize	s	utiz
utilized	s	utid
utilizing	s	utig
utlization	s	utih
vary	smp	vry
variety	s	vary
various	s	vars
vast	smp	vst
verbal	s	vrb
verbally	sm (vrly)	vrby
very	smp	v

victim	smp	vic
victimize	s	vicz
victimized	s	vicd
wait	smp	wt
waited	s	wtd
waiter	s	wtr
waiting	s	wtg
want	smp	wnt
wanted	s	wntd
wanting	s	wntg
was	smp	ws
water	s	watr
we	smp	w
week	smp	wk
well	smp	wl
were	smp	wr
what	smp	wh
wheat	smp	wht
when	smp	whn
where	smp	whr
whether	smp	whtr
which	smp	whh
while	smp	whl
will	smp	wl
willing	s	wilg
wish	smp	wsh
with	smp	wth
within	c	w/in
without	c	w/ou
word	smp	wrd
work	smp	wrk
worked	s	wrkd
worker	s	wrkr

working	s	wrkg
world	smp	wld
would	smp	wd
write	smp	wrt
writer	s	wrtr
writing	s	wrtg
written	smp	writ
yearn	smp	yrn
yes	smp	ys
yesterday	smp	yest
you	smp	u
your	smp	yr
youth	smp	yth

NOTES

NOTES

Prefixes		
ac ap as	= **a**	
com con	= **c**	
de dis	= **d**	
en	= **e**	
ex	= **x**	
for fore	= **f**	
im in inter	= **i**	
ir re	= **r**	

per pre pro	= **p**
sub sup super	= **s**
tran trans	= **t**
un under	= **u**
_____	= __
_____	= __
_____	= __
_____	= __

Suffixes		
able ible	= **b**	
age ing	= **g**	
al	= **l**	
ance ence	= **c**	
ant ent ness	= **n**	
ate est ist	= **t**	
cy ly ry ty	= **y**	
ed	= **d**	

er or	= **r**
es less ous	= **s**
ful	= **f**
ic	= **k**
ism ment	= **m**
ive	= **v**
ize	= **z**

sion tion	= **h**
ship	= **p**
ure	= **u**
_____	= __
_____	= __
_____	= __
_____	= __
_____	= __

161

NOTES

Prefixes					Suffixes				
ac ap as	= **a**	per pre pro	= **p**	able ible	= **b**	er or	= **r**	sion tion	= **h**
com con	= **c**	sub sup super	= **s**	age ing	= **g**	es less ous	= **s**	ship	= **p**
de dis	= **d**	tran trans	= **t**	al	= **l**	ful	= **f**	ure	= **u**
en	= **e**	un under	= **u**	ance ence	= **c**	ic	= **k**	_____	= __
ex	= **x**	_____	= __	ant ent ness	= **n**	ism ment	= **m**	_____	= __
for fore	= **f**	_____	= __	ate est ist	= **t**	ive	= **v**	_____	= __
im in inter	= **i**	_____	= __	cy ly ry ty	= **y**	ize	= **z**	_____	= __
ir re	= **r**	_____	= __	ed	= **d**		= __	_____	= __

NOTES

Prefixes						Suffixes					
ac ap as	= **a**	per pre pro	= **p**	able ible	= **b**	er or	= **r**	sion tion	= **h**
com con	= **c**	sub sup super	= **s**	age ing	= **g**	es less ous	= **s**	ship	= **p**
de dis	= **d**	tran trans	= **t**	al	= **l**	ful	= **f**	ure	= **u**
en	= **e**	un under	= **u**	ance ence	= **c**	ic	= **k**	_____	= __
ex	= **x**	_____	= __	ant ent ness	= **n**	ism ment	= **m**	_____	= __
for fore	= **f**	_____	= __	ate est ist	= **t**	ive	= **v**	_____	= __
im in inter	= **i**	_____	= __	cy ly ry ty	= **y**	ize	= **z**	_____	= __
ir re	= **r**	_____	= __	ed	= **d**	_____	= __	_____	= __

NOTES

Prefixes				Suffixes			
ac ap as	= **a**	per pre pro	= **p**	able ible = **b**	er or	= **r**	sion tion = **h**
com con	= **c**	sub sup super	= **s**	age ing = **g**	es less ous	= **s**	ship	= **p**
de dis	= **d**	tran trans	= **t**	al = **l**	ful	= **f**	ure	= **u**
en	= **e**	un under	= **u**	ance ence = **c**	ic	= **k**	_____	= __
ex	= **x**	_____	= __	ant ent ness= **n**	ism ment	= **m**	_____	= __
for fore	= **f**	_____	= __	ate est ist = **t**	ive	= **v**	_____	= __
im in inter	= **i**	_____	= __	cy ly ry ty = **y**	ize	= **z**	_____	= __
ir re	= **r**	_____	= __	ed = **d**		= __	_____	= __